Christmas Recipes

a Collecting & Sharing Journal
with pockets

Amherst Press
a division of Palmer Publications, Inc.
Amherst, Wisconsin

Copyright © 1999 Amherst Press

First Edition

BOOK ISBN: 0-942495-68-3
RECIPE CARD ISBN: 0-942495-90-X

Published by
Amherst Press
a division of Palmer Publications, Inc.
318 North Main Street
Amherst, Wisconsin 54406

Printed in the United States of America by
Palmer Publications, Inc.

Designed and marketed by Amherst Press
Christmas Recipes is a companion book to
Collecting & Sharing Recipes

Cover art and illustrations by
Paige Houghton
Houghton Art Studio
Amherst, Wisconsin 54406

This book is dedicated to all those who cherish
Christmas recipes and traditions, realizing they are
the ribbon that connects generations of families,
and who wish to preserve them
for the generations to come.

How to Use This Book

This holiday season, simplify your life with
Christmas Recipes, a Collecting & Sharing Journal with pockets.
All the necessary ingredients are here: blank pages set up for recipes,
a journal section for special memories, helpful cooking tips and suggestions
at the back of the book, and pockets for…just about anything.
Following are some suggestions for how to use this book.

A Personal Touch

Start your personalized copy by turning back to page *iv*. This blank page
has been designed so that you may make your own dedication page, create an
acknowledgment, or write a message to the person receiving the book as a gift.

Christmas Recipes

As a recipe resource: Imagine—all your favorite Christmas recipes written
down in one book! No more searching through recipe boxes, a dozen cook-
books and a hundred scraps of paper to find that recipe for cranberry sauce
that was such a hit last year. From Great-Grandmother's pumpkin pie to the
kids' favorite sugar cookies, you can keep all your essential Christmas
recipes in one place. The holiday turkey has a place here, as well as
those heavenly side dishes—necessary old standbys as well as
new favorites. The holiday season is such a busy time; be sure
to include a few recipes for make-ahead meals that can go
from freezer to table quickly. You can organize these
recipes in any way you like: cookbook-style (appetizers,
main dishes, desserts), or by family member (Grandma's
recipes, then Aunt Jane's, and so on), or by the calendar
(holiday cookies, to Christmas Eve dinner, to New Year's
Day brunch). Whichever method you choose, log your recipes in
the Contents section starting on page 6. The lined pages to write your recipes
are from page 17-100.

As a family holiday history: Tradition is an inherent part of the holiday
season. Think of **Christmas Recipes** as a family history, defined by food. You
know that recipe you call Mom for every year? Write it down here, and call
Mom just to chat instead. Fill a copy of **Christmas Recipes** with those

precious recipes to pass on to a member of the next generation. They'll keep those cherished memories alive, and create new ones of their own.

As a special holiday gift: Fill the first pages of **Christmas Recipes** with your favorite recipes and create a truly personal gift for one you love—they'll remember you each time they use the book. Send your son or daughter out into the world with all their Christmas memories and traditions lovingly saved in one place (make sure to leave room for them to add new ones of their own). As a hostess gift, or a hard-to-buy present (for a teacher, scout leader, neighbor) **Christmas Recipes** will be cherished for years.

As an ideas book: It's July, and you find a fabulous recipe for flavored vinegar (or herbal blends, or potpourri…); the perfect Christmas present! Jot it down in **Christmas Recipes**, and it's there after Thanksgiving when you're desperate for gift ideas. The pockets (see below) are just right for slipping notes in, as well.

A Place for Christmas Memories

The journal section starting on page 101 is for "remember when" stories—hilarious anecdotes and heart-tugging moments that characterize your family's Christmases. Remember that year you actually saw Santa slipping the presents under the tree, or the time the whole family went caroling in a snowstorm, or when the puppy ran off with the Christmas turkey? The essence of your family is in these stories, and you can preserve them here.

Pockets to Hold Christmas Treasures

A favorite Christmas card, a child's first note to Santa, a snapshot of the family in front of the tree…the pockets are for treasures. Tuck in a recipe for fudge from your best friend, the tag from a very special gift, the words to your favorite carols.

The pockets have practical uses, too. How much time did you spend last year trying to find—or reconstruct—the Christmas card list? This year, tuck it into one of **Christmas Recipes'** pockets. Keep your receipts from your gift purchases—and your gift list, along with appropriate sizes and other helpful notes.

(We've designed recipe cards to coordinate with the book. They're available separately and make a wonderful gift in combination with the book. See page 124.)

Sharing Favorite Christmas Recipes

To get you started, the staff of Amherst Press has shared some of their favorite holiday recipes. They're included and are written in a standard cook's format, one that we've found to be clear and understandable. For example, ingredients are listed in order of use at the top of the page, which helps in preparing your grocery list as well as in preparing the dish. The oven temperature, pan sizes, and cooking times are included, and the recipes are broken into easy steps.

This certainly doesn't mean you should discard those generational recipes that break every rule.(a pinch of this, a handful of that, mix, and cook until done). Those dishes are more essential to a true family Christmas than any gourmet delicacy.

Sharing Helpful Information

In the back, we've included a few charts and tips to make your holiday preparations run a bit more smoothly. Ingredient substitutions, candy thermometer temperatures, and tips on packing and shipping cookies will, we hope, help pave the way to a less hectic holiday. This section is already logged in the Contents.

When planning your holidays
or to pass on your family's traditions,
Christmas Recipes is the one book you will need
for a simply perfect Christmas.

Contents

Contents

Contents

Sharing Favorite Christmas Recipes

recipe name: Caramel Corn
from: Heidi Bittner-Zastrow
yield: 8 quarts

A former co-worker, Kathy White, shared this recipe with me many years ago. This has become a family favorite! Adding walnuts or almonds makes it extra special for gift-giving.

1 1/3 cups popcorn, unpopped
1 cup butter
1/2 cup Karo syrup, white
1 teaspoon salt (optional)

1 teaspoon vanilla
1/2 teaspoon baking soda
Nuts (optional)

Pop popcorn in 2 batches, using 2/3 cup each time. Place popped corn into a large roasting pan. Nuts can be added if desired.

Combine butter, Karo syrup, salt and vanilla in a large saucepan. Bring to a boil and boil for 5 minutes.

Remove from heat, add baking soda, and mix well. Pour over popcorn and mix well.

Bake at 250° for 1 hour, stirring often. Remove from oven and stir occasionally to prevent clumping.

recipe name: Cranberry Apple Salad with Lime Vinaigrette

from: THE SUNDAY COOK cookbook by Grace Howaniec

yield: serves 8 (leftovers are so good that I usually double the recipe)

1½ cups cranberries

4 TBSP. plus 2 tsp. sugar

1 tsp. orange zest

2 TBSP. lime juice

2 tsp. Dijon mustard

½ c. olive or vegetable oil

2 large Granny Smith apples, chopped

1 c. chopped walnuts

¼ c. sliced green onions

½ c. golden raisins

1 head romaine lettuce

Coarsely chop cranberries. Place in bowl with 4 TBSP. sugar and orange zest; cover and refrigerate overnight.

Using a blender, combine lime juice, mustard and remaining 2 tsp. sugar. Gradually add olive oil blending until smooth. Combine apples, walnuts, onions and raisins in a medium bowl. Pour vinaigrette over mixture and stir to blend. Refrigerate 1 hour or overnight.

To serve, line a platter with torn romaine leaves. Spoon apple mixture onto romaine leaving a border of lettuce. Make a small well in center of apple mixture and add cranberry mixture. Garnish with additional lime zest, if desired.

recipe name: Sweet Potatoes with maple Syrup
from: Connie Halverson
yield: 8-10 Servings

4-5   sweet potatoes
4 T.   butter, divided
1/4 C.   maple syrup
1 tsp.   grated orange peel
1/2 tsp. salt
1/4 C.   chopped pecans

Boil potatoes partly covered for 20 minutes or until just tender; drain, peel and quarter. Melt 2T. butter in baking dish, arrange potatoes.

Heat remaining 2 T butter in a saucepan with syrup, orange peel and salt. Cook until bubbly (3-4 min.) Pour over potatoes. Bake at 350° for 5 minutes, turn potatoes, add pecans and cook 15 minutes.

recipe name: <u>Norwegian Rice Pudding</u>
from: <u>Marcia Leenzen</u>
yield: <u>6-8 servings</u>

Serve in a crystal bowl and let
everyone help themselves. Whoever
receives the almond in their serving
will have good luck in the coming
year.

    1½ cups uncooked white rice
    1   cup water
    ½ cup golden raisins
    ¼ teaspoon allspice
    ½ teaspoon vanilla
    ¼ stick butter
    1 8-oz. container whipping cream
    ¾ cup sugar
    1 whole almond

Place all ingredients, except cream
and sugar, in covered baking dish,
and bake at 350° until rice is done.
(45 minutes to 1 hour).

Beat cream, folding in sugar, until
stiff peaks form. Fold into rice right
before serving -- along with the almond!

Serve warm with choice of topping;
sugar, cinnamon, or homemade lingonberry
sauce.

recipe name: Chocolate Crinkles
from: Nancy Root Miller
yield: about 7 dozen cookies

½ cup vegetable oil
2 cups sugar
4 ounces unsweetened
  chocolate, melted
2 tsp. vanilla

2 cups flour
2 tsp. baking powder
½ tsp. salt
1½ cups confectioner's
  sugar

In a large bowl, mix oil, sugar and chocolate.
Add eggs 1 at a time, beating well after each one.
Add vanilla. Stir in flour, baking powder and salt;
mix well. Cover bowl & refrigerate several hours.
   Put confectioner's sugar in a shallow bowl. Roll
teaspoonfuls of chilled dough in balls; roll balls
in confectioner's sugar. Bake at 350° for 8-9
minutes – do not overbake.

The snowy sugar coating cracks as the cookies
bake, revealing the rich chocolate underneath.
My Mom makes these treats every year at
Christmas, and now I do, too.

Christmas Recipes

recipe name: _____

from: _____

yield: _____

recipe name: _____

from: _____

yield: _____

recipe name: _____

from: _____

yield: _____

_____
_____
_____
_____
_____
_____
_____
_____
_____
_____
_____
_____
_____
_____
_____
_____
_____
_____
_____
_____
_____
_____
_____
_____
_____
_____
_____

recipe name: _____

from: _____

yield: _____

recipe name: _____

from: _____

yield: _____

recipe name: _____

from: _____

yield: _____

recipe name: _____

from: _____

yield: _____

_____
_____
_____
_____
_____
_____
_____
_____
_____
_____
_____
_____
_____
_____
_____
_____
_____
_____
_____
_____
_____
_____
_____
_____

recipe name: _____

from: _____

yield: _____

_____
_____
_____
_____
_____
_____
_____
_____
_____
_____
_____
_____
_____
_____
_____
_____
_____
_____
_____
_____
_____
_____
_____
_____
_____

recipe name: _____

from: _____

yield: _____

recipe name: _____
from: _____
yield: _____

recipe name: _____

from: _____

yield: _____

recipe name: _____

from: _____

yield: _____

recipe name: _____

from: _____

yield: _____

recipe name: _____

from: _____

yield: _____

recipe name: _____

from: _____

yield: _____

recipe name: _____

from: _____

yield: _____

recipe name: _____

from: _____

yield: _____

_____
_____
_____
_____
_____
_____
_____
_____
_____
_____
_____
_____
_____
_____
_____
_____
_____
_____
_____
_____
_____
_____
_____
_____
_____
_____

recipe name: _____

from: _____

yield: _____

_____

_____

_____

_____

_____

_____

_____

_____

_____

_____

_____

_____

_____

_____

_____

_____

_____

_____

_____

_____

_____

_____

_____

_____

_____

recipe name: _____

from: _____

yield: _____

recipe name: _____

from: _____

yield: _____

recipe name: _____

from: _____

yield: _____

recipe name: _____

from: _____

yield: _____

recipe name: _____

from: _____

yield: _____

recipe name: _____

from: _____

yield: _____

recipe name: _____

from: _____

yield: _____

recipe name: _____

from: _____

yield: _____

recipe name: _____

from: _____

yield: _____

recipe name: _____

from: _____

yield: _____

recipe name: _____

from: _____

yield: _____

recipe name: _____

from: _____

yield: _____

recipe name: _____

from: _____

yield: _____

recipe name: _____

from: _____

yield: _____

_____

_____

_____

_____

_____

_____

_____

_____

_____

_____

_____

_____

_____

_____

_____

_____

_____

_____

_____

_____

_____

_____

_____

recipe name: _____

from: _____

yield: _____

recipe name: _____

from: _____

yield: _____

recipe name: _____

from: _____

yield: _____

recipe name: _____

from: _____

yield: _____

_____

_____

_____

_____

_____

_____

_____

_____

_____

_____

_____

_____

_____

_____

_____

_____

_____

_____

_____

_____

_____

_____

_____

_____

_____

_____

_____

recipe name: _____

from: _____

yield: _____

_____

_____

_____

_____

_____

_____

_____

_____

_____

_____

_____

_____

_____

_____

_____

_____

_____

_____

_____

_____

_____

_____

_____

_____

_____

recipe name: _____

from: _____

yield: _____

recipe name: _____

from: _____

yield: _____

recipe name: _____

from: _____

yield: _____

recipe name: _____

from: _____

yield: _____

_____
_____
_____
_____
_____
_____
_____
_____
_____
_____
_____
_____
_____
_____
_____
_____
_____
_____
_____
_____
_____
_____
_____
_____
_____
_____
_____

recipe name: _____

from: _____

yield: _____

_____
_____
_____
_____
_____
_____
_____
_____
_____
_____
_____
_____
_____
_____
_____
_____
_____
_____
_____
_____
_____
_____
_____
_____
_____
_____
_____

recipe name: _____

from: _____

yield: _____

recipe name: _____

from: _____

yield: _____

recipe name: _____

from: _____

yield: _____

recipe name: _____

from: _____

yield: _____

_____
_____
_____
_____
_____
_____
_____
_____
_____
_____
_____
_____
_____
_____
_____
_____
_____
_____
_____
_____
_____
_____
_____
_____

recipe name: _____

from: _____

yield: _____

recipe name: _____

from: _____

yield: _____

recipe name: _____

from: _____

yield: _____

_____
_____
_____
_____
_____
_____
_____
_____
_____
_____
_____
_____
_____
_____
_____
_____
_____
_____
_____
_____
_____
_____
_____
_____
_____
_____

recipe name: _____

from: _____

yield: _____

_____

_____

_____

_____

_____

_____

_____

_____

_____

_____

_____

_____

_____

_____

_____

_____

_____

_____

_____

_____

_____

_____

_____

_____

recipe name: _____

from: _____

yield: _____

recipe name: _____

from: _____

yield: _____

_____
_____
_____
_____
_____
_____
_____
_____
_____
_____
_____
_____
_____
_____
_____
_____
_____
_____
_____
_____
_____
_____
_____
_____
_____

recipe name: _____

from: _____

yield: _____

_____

_____

_____

_____

_____

_____

_____

_____

_____

_____

_____

_____

_____

_____

_____

_____

_____

_____

_____

_____

_____

_____

recipe name: _____

from: _____

yield: _____

recipe name: _____

from: _____

yield: _____

_____
_____
_____
_____
_____
_____
_____
_____
_____
_____
_____
_____
_____
_____
_____
_____
_____
_____
_____
_____
_____
_____
_____
_____
_____

recipe name: _____

from: _____

yield: _____

recipe name: _____

from: _____

yield: _____

recipe name: _____

from: _____

yield: _____

_____

_____

_____

_____

_____

_____

_____

_____

_____

_____

_____

_____

_____

_____

_____

_____

_____

_____

_____

_____

_____

_____

_____

_____

_____

recipe name: _____

from: _____

yield: _____

_____
_____
_____
_____
_____
_____
_____
_____
_____
_____
_____
_____
_____
_____
_____
_____
_____
_____
_____
_____
_____
_____
_____
_____
_____

recipe name: _____

from: _____

yield: _____

_____

_____

_____

_____

_____

_____

_____

_____

_____

_____

_____

_____

_____

_____

_____

_____

_____

_____

_____

_____

_____

_____

_____

_____

recipe name: _____

from: _____

yield: _____

recipe name: _____

from: _____

yield: _____

recipe name: _____

from: _____

yield: _____

recipe name: _____

from: _____

yield: _____

_____
_____
_____
_____
_____
_____
_____
_____
_____
_____
_____
_____
_____
_____
_____
_____
_____
_____
_____
_____
_____
_____
_____
_____
_____

recipe name: _____

from: _____

yield: _____

recipe name: _____

from: _____

yield: _____

recipe name: _____

from: _____

yield: _____

recipe name: _____

from: _____

yield: _____

recipe name: _____

from: _____

yield: _____

recipe name: _____

from: _____

yield: _____

recipe name: _____
from: _____
yield: _____

recipe name: _____

from: _____

yield: _____

_____
_____
_____
_____
_____
_____
_____
_____
_____
_____
_____
_____
_____
_____
_____
_____
_____
_____
_____
_____
_____
_____
_____
_____
_____

recipe name: _____
from: _____
yield: _____

_____
_____
_____
_____
_____
_____
_____
_____
_____
_____
_____
_____
_____
_____
_____
_____
_____
_____
_____
_____
_____
_____
_____
_____
_____
_____

recipe name: _____
from: _____
yield: _____

_____
_____
_____
_____
_____
_____
_____
_____
_____
_____
_____
_____
_____
_____
_____
_____
_____
_____
_____
_____
_____
_____
_____
_____
_____
_____
_____

recipe name: _____

from: _____

yield: _____

recipe name: _____

from: _____

yield: _____

recipe name: _____

from: _____

yield: _____

recipe name: _____

from: _____

yield: _____

recipe name: _____

from: _____

yield: _____

_____
_____
_____
_____
_____
_____
_____
_____
_____
_____
_____
_____
_____
_____
_____
_____
_____
_____
_____
_____
_____
_____
_____
_____
_____
_____
_____
_____
_____
_____
_____

recipe name: _____

from: _____

yield: _____

recipe name: _____

from: _____

yield: _____

_____
_____
_____
_____
_____
_____
_____
_____
_____
_____
_____
_____
_____
_____
_____
_____
_____
_____
_____
_____
_____
_____
_____
_____
_____
_____
_____

recipe name: _____

from: _____

yield: _____

recipe name: _____

from: _____

yield: _____

A Place for Christmas Memories

Sharing
Helpful
Information

Cookies

We often signal the beginning of the holiday season by baking cookies to have on hand for company, to give as gifts, or just to enjoy. The simple pleasure of cookies seems especially suited to the Christmas season. Elegant madeleines and delicate lace cookies are sophisticated enough for a dinner party; frosted sugar cookies are perfect for gatherings for children. From tiny melt-in-your-mouth morsels to giant "monster" cookies, these treats come in every size and shape. Whatever kind your family enjoys, cookies are an inseparable part of the holidays.

Bar cookies are generally quick and easy to make—prepare the dough, spread in the pan and bake. Bars can be served right from the pan, making them convenient for potlucks and traveling. They can be cut into novelty shapes for an easy, creative presentation. There are countless recipes for bars, including a myriad of variations on the best-known bar, the brownie. Layered bar cookies, simple to make and rich and luxurious to eat, often start with a crumb crust and add delectable fillings, such as caramel, chocolate, nuts, or fruit. Some like their bars chewy, some crumbly, some gooey and hot right from the oven.

Drop cookies are made by dropping spoonfuls of dough onto baking sheets. Some are then flattened with a fork or the bottom of a glass dipped in sugar. Easy-to-do, popular drop cookies include chocolate chip, peanut butter, and oatmeal. Cookies will bake uniformly if they are the same size. To keep cookies from spreading, chill the dough before dropping on baking sheets. Whenever possible, bake only one batch of cookies at a time, in the center of the oven, so the heat can circulate evenly. Always let baking pans cool completely between batches.

Rolled cookies are a child's holiday favorite. Frosted sugar cookies are the classic Christmas choice. Children love making sugar cookies, cutting them in their favorite shapes, and decorating them with colored icings, sprinkles, and tiny candies. For great family fun, personalize gingerbread men; save the best ones to hang on the tree. Who doesn't have the memory of decorating gingerbread men by dropping just the right amount of food coloring into bowls of icing? For best results only lightly flour the rolling pin and rolling surface, as too much flour toughens the cookies. Be sure the dough is rolled to a uniform thickness so cookies will bake evenly. Watch cookies as they bake, using the least amount of time necessary, creating a lightly browned, crisp yet tender cookie.

Refrigerator (or icebox) cookies are made by rolling the dough into a log, wrapping it well, and refrigerating or freezing until the dough is ready to be sliced and baked. As with other types of cookies, these can be made in a wide range of flavors. The end result is a batch of delicious, uniformly sized cookies which look pretty and pack well.

Whether they are bar, drop, rolled, or refrigerator, cookies make great gifts. Pack them in decorative tins or recycled glass jars, tied with ribbon or raffia. Think creatively—how about a clean flowerpot, or a pretty ceramic bowl? For a coffee or tea devotee, send their favorite beverage along with a pair of mugs filled with biscotti for dipping.

To ship cookies, always start with a sturdy box. Pairs of cookies can be wrapped with flat undersides together. For a large assortment, place the heaviest cookies at the bottom and the more fragile ones on top, separating the layers with waxed paper. Wrap like cookies together so the flavors won't mingle. Line your packing box with a layer of bubble wrap or crumpled paper, and cover the packed cookies with the same material. Use plain popped popcorn to fill spaces around packed cookies.

As gifts or to enjoy at home with your family,
cookies are an essential part of the Christmas season.

Candies

Tucked into a stocking, displayed in a lovely dish, or wrapped for a gift, candies are always a treat at Christmas. From simple squares of fudge to marzipan in fantastic shapes, candies are a special indulgence at the holidays.

When making candies with a boiled sugar syrup base, always begin with a heavy saucepan at least four times the volume of your ingredients so that the mixture will not boil over. Bring the liquid called for in your recipe to a boil. Remove the pan from the heat, add the sugar, and stir until dissolved. Return the pan to the heat, cover, and cook for two to three minutes, until the mixture is boiling and steam has washed the sugar crystals from the sides of the pan. It is important to let the steam do the work; if you scrape the crystals from the sides into the boiling syrup, you'll have a grainy mess.

Once the sides are clear, uncover the saucepan and continue cooking; do not stir at any time. Position your candy thermometer, if using, in the saucepan and start checking the temperature. In general, sugar syrup will need longer cooking times on humid days than on dry days.

Once the syrup has reached the desired temperature, cool it by immediately placing the saucepan into a pan of ice water, being careful not to disturb the syrup. Alternatively, you can very carefully pour the hot syrup onto a large buttered marble slab or stoneware platter. Do not scrape the pan. In either case, let the syrup cool to 110 degrees before working it.

Stage	Temperature	Description
Thread	230°–234° F	Drop a small amount into ice water and a coarse thread will form.
Soft ball	234°–240° F	Drop a small amount into ice water and a ball will form and flatten out when picked up with the fingers.
Firm ball	242°–248° F	Drop a small amount into ice water and a ball will form that holds its own shape and will not flatten unless pressed with fingers.
Hard ball	250°–268° F	Drop a small amount into ice water and a ball will form which holds its shape yet is still pliable.
Soft crack	270°–290° F	Drop a small amount into ice water and it will separate into hard threads which can be bent and will not be brittle when removed from water.
Hard crack	300°–310° F	Drop a small amount into ice water and it will separate into threads that are hard and brittle.
Caramelized sugar	310°–338° F	Syrup will turn dark golden.

Standard Temperatures for Roasted Meats

(internal temperature when removed from oven*)

Beef
    rare 120°–125° F
    medium rare 130°–140° F
    medium 145°–150° F
    well done 155°–165° F

Veal
    well done 155°–160° F

Lamb
    rare 130°–135° F
    medium rare 140°–145° F
    medium 150°–160° F
    well done 160°–165°F

Pork
    fresh 155°–160° F
    cured (uncooked) 140°–150° F
    cured (ready to eat) 130° F

Poultry
    chicken 180°–185° F
    turkey 180°–185° F

*Meat will continue cooking after it is removed from the oven, causing the internal temperature to rise by approximately 5 degrees. The above temperatures are based on this fact; all roasted meats should rest at least 15 minutes before carving or up to 30 minutes for larger roasts.

Ingredient Substitutions

ingredient	substitute
Butter	
2 sticks (1/2 pound)	7/8 cup vegetable oil
2 sticks (1/2 pound)	7/8 cup lard
Eggs	
1 whole egg	2 egg yolks plus 1 tablespoon water (for use in baking)
2 egg yolks	1 whole egg (for custards, mayonnaise, other sauces)
Flour	
1 cup all-purpose flour	1 cup plus 2 tablespoons cake flour
1 cup cake flour	7/8 cup (1 cup less 2 tablespoons) all-purpose flour
1 cup self-rising flour	1 cup all-purpose flour plus 1 1/4 teaspoons baking powder and a pinch of salt
Leavening	
1 teaspoon double-acting baking powder	1/4 teaspoon baking baking soda plus 1/2 teaspoon cream of tartar
1 envelope (1/4 ounce) dry yeast	1 scant tablespoon dry yeast
1 small cake (0.6 ounce) fresh yeast	1 envelope dry yeast
1 large cake (2 ounces) fresh yeast	3 small (0.6 ounce) cakes fresh or 3 envelopes (1/4 ounce each) dry yeast
Milk and Cream	
1 cup whole milk	1 cup skim milk plus 2 teaspoons melted butter
1 cup fresh milk	1/2 cup evaporated milk plus 1/2 cup water

ingredient	*substitute*
1 cup fresh milk	1/3 cup nonfat dry milk plus 3/4 cup water plus 2 teaspoons melted butter
1 cup fresh milk	1 cup sour cream or buttermilk plus 1/2 teaspoon baking soda
1 cup skim milk	1/3 cup nonfat dry milk plus 3/4 cup water
1 cup light cream	3/4 cup milk plus 3 tablespoons melted butter
1 cup sour cream	1 cup plain yogurt
1 cup sour cream	1 cup evaporated milk plus 1 tablespoon lemon juice

Sweeteners

1 cup granulated sugar	7/8 cup honey
1 cup granulated sugar	1 cup maple syrup plus 1/4 cup corn syrup
1 cup light corn syrup or honey	1 1/4 cups granulated sugar plus 1/3 cup liquid
1 cup granulated sugar	1 cup molasses plus 1 teaspoon baking soda

Thickening Agents

1 tablespoon cornstarch	2 tablespoons all-purpose flour
1 tablespoon potato flour	2 tablespoons all-purpose flour
1 tablespoon tapioca	1 1/2 tablespoons all-purpose flour

To order copies of this book or companion recipe cards,
or for a complete catalog of books published by Amherst Press
call 1-800-333-8122 or
e-mail us at: amherstpress@palmerpublications.com
Secure, encrypted website shopping at: http://www.AmherstPress.com

Merry Christmas

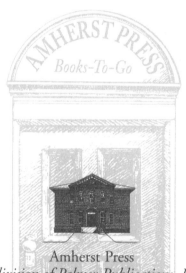

Amherst Press
a division of Palmer Publications, Inc.

PO Box 296
Amherst, WI 54406